PART ONE
THE GREAT POWERS OF OLD EUROPE

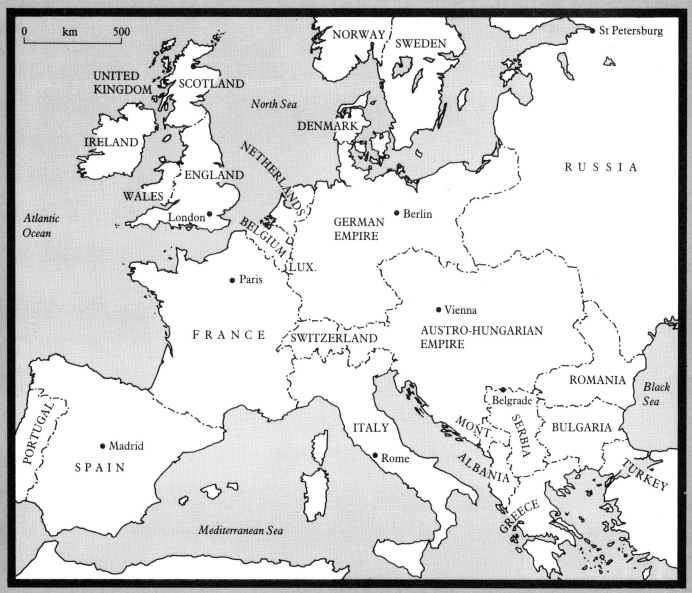

Europe in 1914

At half past two in the night of 3 August 1914, a crowded train stood waiting to leave the Vaugirard station in Paris. Every compartment was packed with fully equipped soldiers waiting to go to war. As they waited nervously for the train to move off, one of them wrote this in his diary:

> '2.30 a.m. Where shall we be tomorrow? How many of us will be alive a month from now? And how many . . . will return and march in the victory parade amidst the applause of the crowds?'

The answers to his questions were more terrible than he could imagine. A month later, many of the men on that train were already dead. The survivors did not return for four years, and few were able to march in any victory parade. For during those four years over six million were wounded and another million went missing, never to be seen again. The soldier writing in his diary was being taken to fight in the most awful war the world had ever known – the Great War of 1914 to 1918.

This book tells the story of how the Great War began. Part One provides you with evidence about the five greatest powers of old Europe – Britain, Germany, Austria-Hungary, Russia and France. You should study this evidence and do the work on page 12 before going any further – for these were the countries that went to war in 1914.

1

1

GREAT BRITAIN – AN ISLAND EMPIRE

Background

Great Britain is a small country but at the start of this century she was the greatest of the world's great powers. Under Queen Victoria (1837–1901) Britain had become the richest and most powerful nation on earth. She had the richest industries, the most trade, the largest number of colonies and the biggest navy.

You probably know the song 'Land of Hope and Glory'. It was written in 1901 and sums up what many British people felt about their country at that time:

> 'Land of Hope and Glory, Mother of the Free,
> How shall we extol thee, who are born of thee?
> Wider still and wider shall thy bounds be set;
> God who made thee mighty, make thee mightier yet.'

Great Britain's ruler

Name King George V
Reign 1910 – 36
Character The man who ruled the greatest country in the world was shy and quiet. He spent fifteen years in the Royal Navy before becoming King in 1910, aged 45. Unlike his father he was a devoted family man. There was nothing very unusual about him except that, as one historian has pointed out, his trousers were creased at the sides, not back to front. In comparison with many rulers of the time, King George had little power. He could not make his own laws, for British monarchs can only make laws which have been drawn up by Parliament.

Britain's pride: crowds gather to watch the Royal Navy on show at Spithead in 1914

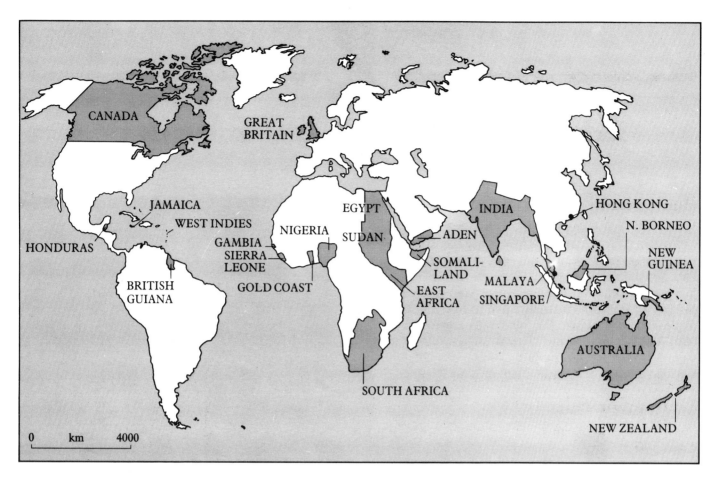

The British Empire

King George V was not only the ruler of Great Britain but also the Emperor of India and ruler of many other lands overseas. These colonies formed the British Empire, the largest empire in the world. If you look at this map you can see that the British Empire took up nearly a quarter of the world's land surface. One quarter of the world's population lived in the British Empire. This is one reason why Britain, a small island nation, was the greatest power in the world in 1900. Study the table below and think about how such a large population helped Britain to be powerful.

Statistics for 1914

Population of Britain	40.8 million
Population of the colonies	390 million
Number of British colonies	56
Size of the British colonies	27 million sq.km.
Britain's army	700,000 soldiers
Britain's navy	388 ships
Coal output each year	292 million tonnes
Steel output each year	11 million tonnes

Problems

Britain may have been a 'Land of Hope and Glory', but she also had a number of problems. Unemployment was rising. Workers in powerful trade unions were organising strikes. Riots and demonstrations were becoming common.

The biggest problem facing Britain was what to do with Ireland. Ireland was part of Great Britain and was governed from London. But most Irish people wanted to change this. They wanted to break away from Britain and have Home Rule. Protestants living in the North, however, wanted to stay British. By 1914, both Protestants and Home Rulers were armed and ready to fight. It looked as if there would be a civil war in Ireland.

Which of the two sides do you think issued this poster? Give reasons for your answer

GERMANY – A NEW EMPIRE

Background

In 1914 Germany was less than fifty years old. Before 1870 there was no such country, only a collection of small states, each with its own ruler. One of the states, Prussia, was bigger than the rest: its ruler wanted to join up with the others to get more land and power. Nearby France and Austria wanted to stop this and so made war on Prussia. But both were beaten and in 1871 Prussia united the German states into a new country – the German Empire. You can see where the German Empire was on the map on page 1.

Germany's ruler

Name Kaiser Wilhelm II
Reign 1888 – 1918
Character Kaiser Wilhelm was King George V's cousin but was the exact opposite in character. He was very energetic and had a strong, outgoing personality. Although he was born with a withered left arm, he was an excellent horseman who could also swim, shoot, fence and hunt. Just as his cousin George spent his youth in the navy, so Wilhelm spent most of his youth in the army. When he grew up he loved the army and enjoyed dressing up in military uniform. He could be very charming and friendly but was often impatient and rude. He was very popular with his subjects.

Can you think of any evidence to suggest that Wilhelm posed very carefully for this photograph?

Britain's pride was her navy: Germany's pride was her army. Here Kaiser Wilhelm with a group of German officers in their Pickelhaube helmets try out new military equipment

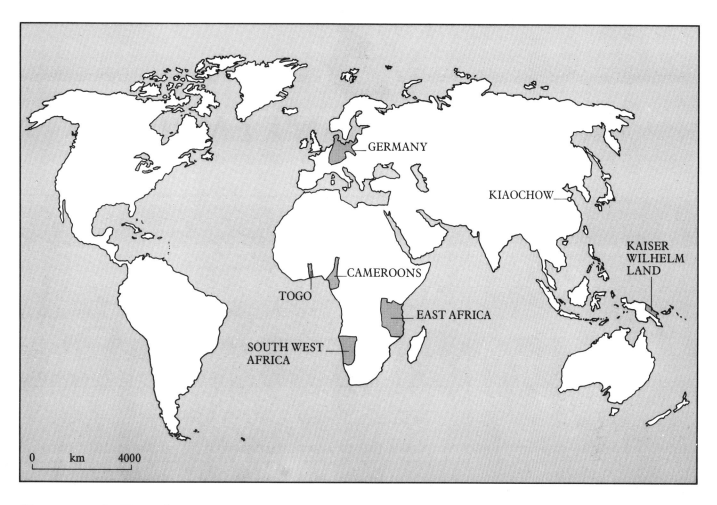

Germany's Empire

Kaiser Wilhelm was jealous of the mighty British Empire. He decided that Germany too must have colonies overseas. He once said that Germany must have 'a place in the sun' and that his aim was 'world-wide power'.

Study this map of Germany's colonies, then say what you think he meant by 'a place in the sun'.

Statistics for 1914

Population of Germany	65 million
Population of the colonies	15 million
Number of German colonies	10
Size of the German colonies	2.5 million sq. km.
Germany's army	4,200,000 soldiers
Germany's navy	281 ships
Coal output each year	277 million tonnes
Steel output each year	14 million tonnes

Problems

Like Britain, Germany too had her problems. Many workers were unhappy because their wages were low, food was expensive and working conditions were bad. More and more workers were joining trade unions and organising strikes, hoping that this would force the government to improve their conditions. Many were also joining the Socialist Party which wanted Kaiser Wilhelm to share his power with Germany's parliament. Some Socialists wanted to overthrow him in a revolution.

But Kaiser Wilhelm did little to improve the conditions of the workers and he refused to share his power. By 1914 one German in every three supported the Socialist Party and many were actively working to start a revolution.

This cartoon shows Kaiser Wilhelm being attacked by a 'socialist dragon'. Why do you think he looks so worried?

5

RUSSIA – A GIANT EMPIRE

Tsar Nicholas with his son, 1911

Can you tell from this map why so many of Russia's riches were not being used?

Background

Russia is the largest country in the world but, in 1900, she was also one of the poorest. She was very rich in minerals – oil, coal, iron ore, gold, etc – but these were not much used. She had a huge population but most people lived in the western half of the country. Hardly anyone at all lived in Siberia. Russia had great amounts of land but much of it was too cold for farming. She had a long coastline but most of it was frozen for half the year, making sea transport impossible. And Russia was an empire of many peoples, each speaking a different language, from the Finns in the north to the Caucasians in the south and the Poles in the west. All these things made Russia hard to govern. The Russian Empire was a very weak 'giant'.

How could Russia, the weak giant, be strengthened? The Tsar hoped that the Trans-Siberian railway would provide at least part of the answer. It was opened in 1901, linking Moscow with Vladivostock, a distance of nearly 10,000 kilometres. (See map above.)

Russia's ruler

Name Tsar Nicholas II
Reign 1894 – 1917
Character Tsar Nicholas II was a weak man and not very clever. He was a bad judge of people and was easily influenced by poor advisers. The worst of these was a monk, Gregory Rasputin. Rasputin had hypnotic powers of healing over Nicholas's son, who had the incurable blood disease haemophilia. Nicholas's greatest weakness was to try to rule Russia as an autocrat. This means that he had complete control of the country and would not share his power. He believed that God had chosen him to rule in this way. This made him unpopular with many of his subjects who believed in democracy, and wanted a say in how their country was governed.

The Trans-Siberian railway

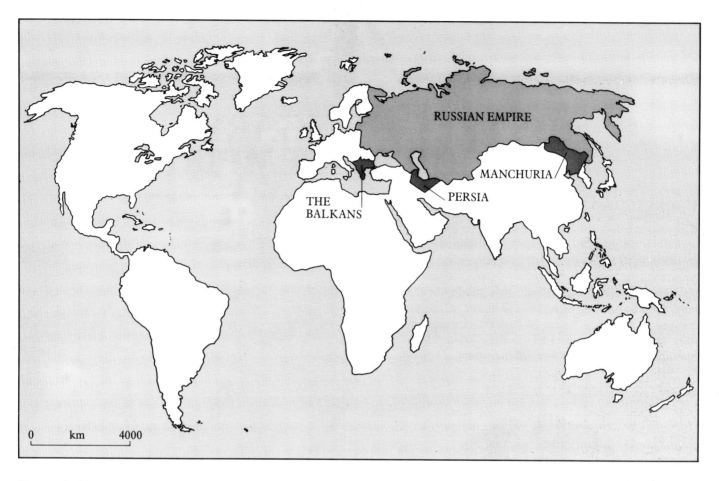

Russia's place in the world

As you can see from this map Russia had no overseas colonies. But Tsar Nicholas did want to get more land beyond his borders. The areas in which he was interested are shaded on the map above.

What do you think Nicholas hoped to gain by taking over these areas? Why should he want to make the largest country in the world even bigger? When thinking of your answer, bear in mind that all three areas were to the south of Russia and that two of them are on seas that do not freeze in winter.

Statistics for 1914

Population of Russia	159 million
Coal output each year	36.2 million tonnes
Steel output each year	3.6 million tonnes
Russia's army	1,200,000 soldiers
Russia's navy	166 ships

Problems

Most Russians lived and worked in dreadful conditions. Workers in the towns laboured for up to fourteen hours a day for very low wages. Their homes were crowded and unhealthy. Workers like these had little reason to support the Tsar. Many were ready to rebel against him.

Nearly eight out of ten Russians were peasants who scraped a living by farming small plots of land. At the best of times, life was hard and short for the peasants. In bad times, when the harvest was poor, many died while others lived desperately close to starvation. Like the workers in the towns, the peasants were ready to rebel against the rule of the Tsar.

Left: What evidence is there in this photograph of a canteen in Moscow at the turn of the century to show you that life for Russian town workers was poor and unhealthy?

AUSTRIA–HUNGARY – A PATCHWORK EMPIRE

Background

You can tell from its name that Austria-Hungary was actually a union of two separate countries. Inside each country lived many different peoples, or nationalities, each with its own language, its own customs and its own way of life. Like Russia, this made the country very hard to govern, especially as many of the peoples wanted to be independent of Austria-Hungary so that they could rule themselves in their own ways. The 'patchwork' of peoples was falling apart.

Austria-Hungary's ruler

Name Emperor Franz Joseph II
Reign 1848 – 1916
Character At eighty-four, Franz Joseph was the oldest of all Europe's rulers. He was a quiet, serious and religious man, devoted to his work. His long life had been a sad one: his brother Maximilian, the ruler of Mexico, had been killed by rebels, his son Rudolf had committed suicide, and his wife had been stabbed to death by an assassin. And in 1900 he was deeply upset when his nephew, Franz Ferdinand, married beneath him to a Countess named Sophie Chotek.

Franz Joseph was well liked by his subjects, but many people hated the government officials who ran the country.

Right: An example of another nationality with its own language, customs and way of life: these girls come from the province of Bosnia in the south of the Empire. They are wearing their wedding dresses and around their necks are the dowries they will give their husbands – necklaces of valuable coins

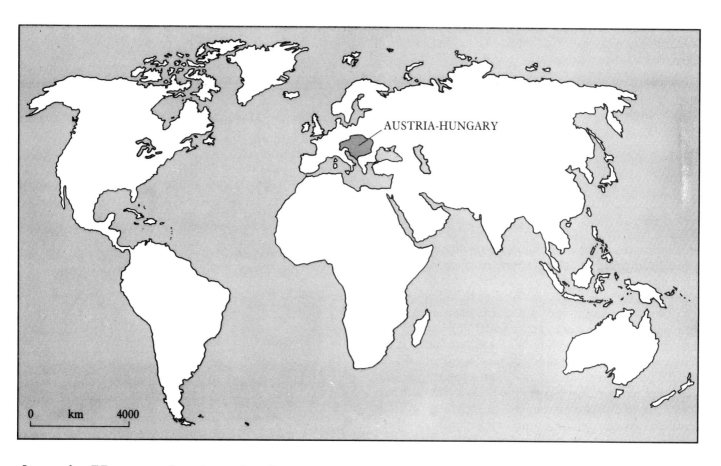

AUSTRIA-HUNGARY

0   km   4000

Austria-Hungary's place in the world

Like Russia, Austria-Hungary had no colonies overseas. Nor did Franz Joseph aim to get any. As you have seen, he already ruled an empire of eleven different nationalities, many of them wanting their freedom. To have colonies overseas would complicate this already serious problem.

Statistics for 1914

Population of Austria-Hungary	50 million
Coal output each year	47 million tonnes
Steel output each year	5 million tonnes
Austria-Hungary's army	800,000 soldiers
Austria-Hungary's navy	67 ships

Problems

By the start of this century the many peoples of Austria-Hungary hated the rule of Franz Joseph's government. This picture drawn in 1897 gives us a good example of the hatred felt by the Czech people living in the province of Bohemia. They are rioting in the streets of Prague, Bohemia's capital city, because the government has just announced that the Czechs will not be allowed to use their own language in schools, newspapers, work places, etc. Instead they will have to use German, the language of the Austrians.

Why do you think the Czech people were so angry about this? And why do you think the Austrian government did not want them to use their own language?

9

5

FRANCE – A REPUBLIC

Background

France was twice the size of Britain and about the same size as Germany. The land was fertile, her people were hard-working, she had an excellent transport system and she owned many colonies. But in spite of these advantages France was weaker than Britain and Germany. Her farms and factories produced less, and her population was not only smaller than theirs but was actually shrinking. Another weakness was that the French people had lost much of their national pride in 1870 when the Germans beat them in the Franco-Prussian War. After this defeat, the Germans took away two valuable provinces from France – Alsace and Lorraine. The loss of these provinces made many French people hate the Germans bitterly.

At the start of the century France was most famous for its artistic life, or culture, and for its fashions. Many of the world's most famous painters, designers, writers, scientists and musicians lived and worked in France. Paris was not only the capital of France, but the cultural capital of the world.

These Parisians are showing off the latest fashions in 1909

France's ruler

Unlike the other great powers of Europe, France was a republic – that is, a country ruled by an elected president, not by a king or queen who inherits the throne.

Name President Raymond Poincaré
Period in office 1913 – 20

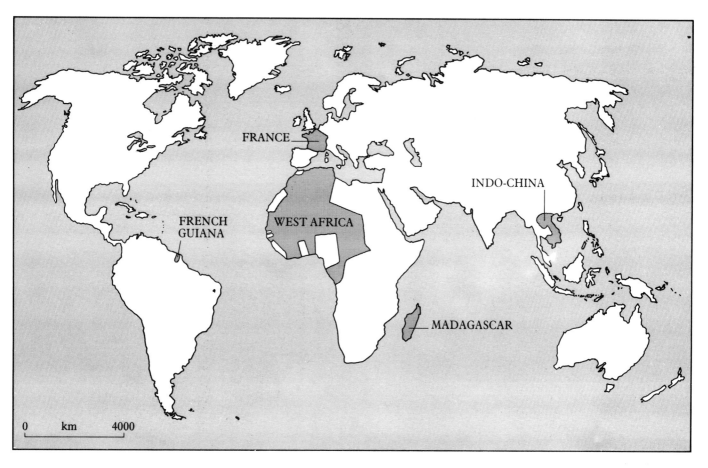

Character Poincaré was a very clever man. Honest and outspoken, sometimes short-tempered, he was also cold and unsympathetic. He was born and brought up in the province of Lorraine. The people of France respected him but they did not like him much. Can you see anything in his character or background to suggest he might be anti-German?

The French Empire

France had the second largest empire in the world. Most of her colonies were in Africa where the French were liked because they built schools, hospitals, roads, ports, etc. Her other main colonies were in the Far East, in Indo-China, and there the French were not at all liked. The French army in Indo-China was often at war with groups of rebels who wanted independence, and the cost of fighting was a drain on France's men and money.

Statistics for 1914

Population of France	39.6 million
Population of the colonies	58 million
Number of French colonies	29
Size of the French colonies	11 million sq. km.
France's army	3,700,000 soldiers
France's navy	207 ships
Coal output each year	40 million tonnes
Steel output each year	4.6 million tonnes

Problems

Until 1870 France was one of the most powerful countries in Europe. But as you have seen, the French felt ashamed when the Prussians beat them in the Franco-Prussian War. Many could remember their grandparents telling them stories of the great victories of Napoleon Bonaparte. Now, not only had the French lost their national pride to the Germans; they had also lost the rich provinces of Alsace and Lorraine. For the next forty years, the French nursed a desire for revenge against the Germans.

Left: In this French cartoon of 1913, a boy stands on a hilltop looking down on the lost provinces of Alsace and Lorraine. The ghosts of French Cavalrymen killed in the Franco-Prussian War gallop through the skies above.

Work section

A. The strength of the great powers

Draw a grid like the one below. Using the statistics for 1914 given in Chapters 1 to 5, fill in the spaces to show the strength of each great power. Then answer the questions beneath.

Country	Britain	Germany	Russia	Austria-Hungary	France
Population					
Number of colonies					
Size of colonies					
Population of colonies					
Size of army					
Size of navy					
Coal output each year					
Steel output each year					

1. a) Which country had the biggest overseas empire in 1914?
   b) Which of the other two overseas empires would you say was stronger than the other? Explain your answer.
2. a) Which country had the biggest army?
   b) Which had the biggest navy?
   c) Can you think of reasons why these countries kept such large armed forces?
3. Which of the five countries had the strongest industry?
4. Which of the five countries had the largest population?
5. Using the evidence above, which country do you think was the leading world power in 1914? Before deciding on an answer, ask yourself what makes a country strong. Is it the size of its army, its industry, its trade, or is it a combination of all these things?

B. The rulers of Europe

1. Here are five statements made by the rulers of the great powers you have studied. Try to work out which ruler made each statement.
   a) 'In the future, no great decisions will be taken without Germany and the German Emperor.'
   b) 'I shall uphold the principle of autocracy just as firmly as it was by my . . . father.'
   c) 'I'm really quite an ordinary sort of chap.'
   d) 'Henceforth the President of the Republic must freely use the powers of which he has been deprived.'
   e) 'My policy is a policy of peace.'
2. a) Which of the rulers you have studied do you think was the most able and why? b) Which do you think was the least able? Explain your answer.

C.
1. Which countries had problems caused by nationalists wanting independence?
2. Why was nationalism a serious problem for these countries?

THE MAKING OF QUARRELS

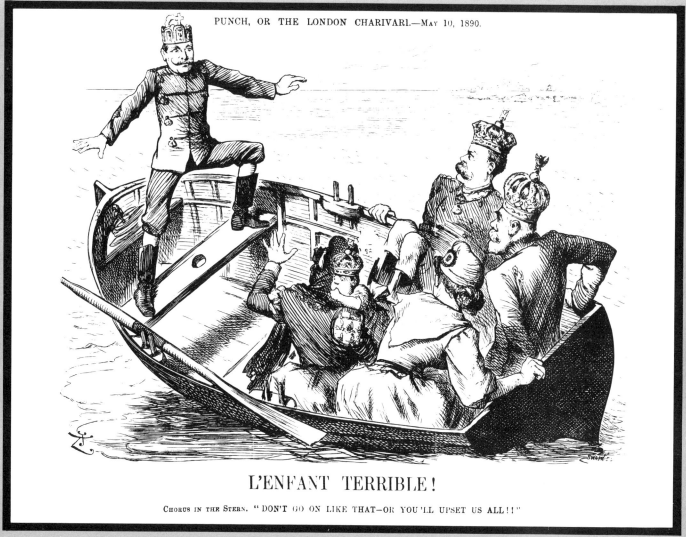

PUNCH, OR THE LONDON CHARIVARI.—MAY 10, 1890.

L'ENFANT TERRIBLE!

CHORUS IN THE STERN. "DON'T GO ON LIKE THAT—OR YOU'LL UPSET US ALL!!"

Kaiser Wilhelm, Emperor of Germany, rocks the boat and alarms his fellow rulers of Europe:
a British cartoon drawn in 1890

You found out in Part One that Europe was dominated by five major powers at the start of this century. Each had great strengths and each had a number of weaknesses. In Part Two you will find that these great powers began to quarrel with each other, more and more angrily as the years went by, until in 1914 their quarrels flared up into a war.

Before you read about the making of their quarrels, ask yourself why any quarrel begins. With individual people, it is easy to understand how an argument starts; one person insulting another can lead to a fight. Neighbours argue about their fences. Football supporters quarrel and sometimes fight about their teams. When we have disagreements like these, our friends become very important to us – we rely on them for loyalty and support.

Much the same sort of thing happens with countries. It is common for the people of one country to think of the people in another country as being either friends or enemies. Today, for example, many Americans see Russians as their enemies but look on the British as friends. These likes and dislikes often change over the years. Two hundred years ago the British and Americans were such bitter enemies that they fought a long war with each other.

Just as ordinary people rely on their friends for support in a quarrel, so do countries. They make agreements to help each other against their common enemies. Such agreements are called alliances.

The first cause of quarrel between the five great powers was to do with the way they made alliances with each other.

6

THE ALLIANCE SYSTEM

Fifty years before the Great War, the likes and dislikes of the European powers were very different from those which existed in 1914.

Britain had no ties with other countries and concentrated instead on building up her empire: Britain was said to be in 'splendid isolation'. The Emperors of Germany, Austria and Russia were tied to each other by an agreement called the 'Three Emperors' League'. France had few friends and was licking her wounds after her defeat in the Franco-Prussian War.

These likes and dislikes started to change in 1879 when Germany quarrelled with Russia. To get protection against a possible Russian attack, Germany agreed with Austria that each would help the other if either of them was attacked.

This agreement was called the **Dual Alliance** and was the first in a series of new friendships that were made before 1914.

It was:

Agreement Number One
The Dual Alliance, 1879
Germany – Austria

Three years later, Italy joined the Dual Alliance making it the **Triple Alliance**:

Agreement Number Two
The Triple Alliance, 1882
Germany – Italy – Austria

This three-way friendship worried France and Russia who both feared that they could be attacked and beaten by three powerful countries acting together. Their fears led to a third alliance. France and Russia agreed in 1892 to help each other if either of them was attacked.

This was the **Franco-Russian Alliance** and, for a while, it calmed the fears of both countries:

Agreement Number Three
The Franco-Russian Alliance, 1892
France – Russia

Now it was Britain's turn to become worried. As you know, Britain had concentrated on building up her empire instead of getting involved with the other European countries. But in one of her colonies, South Africa, Britain fought a war against the Boers, rebel settlers who wanted to be independent. During the Boer War, Germany showed sympathy for the Boers, so the British began to mistrust the Germans and looked for a friend in Europe. In 1903 King Edward of Britain paid a state visit to France and in the following year signed an agreement with France called the **Entente Cordiale**, meaning 'Friendly Under-standing':

Agreement Number Four
The Entente Cordiale, 1904
Britain – France

This meant that Britain was no longer in 'splendid isolation'.

Three years later, in 1907, Britain made a similar agreement with Russia who, as you have seen (Alliance Number Three), was already in alliance with France:

Agreement Number Five
The Triple Entente, 1907
Britain – Russia – France

This agreement was known as the **Triple Entente**.

So by 1907 Europe was clearly divided into two groups:

The Triple Alliance
Germany
Austria-Hungary
Italy

The Triple Entente
Great Britain
France
Russia

As you found out in Part One, the countries in each group were powerful and well armed. If a quarrel started between just two of them, it was certain that the quarrel would quickly spread as they called on their allies for help.

Work section

A. Copy or trace the map below. Give it the title *The Alliances before the Great War*. In one colour, shade the countries which belonged to the Triple Alliance and in another colour shade the members of the Triple Entente. Don't forget to fill in the key to the map.

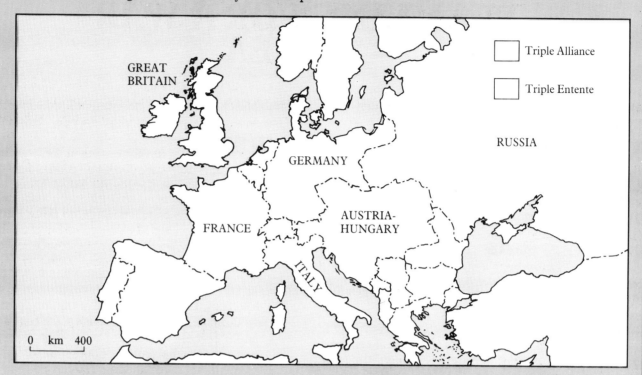

Now answer these questions.
1. If the Triple Alliance attacked France, how could Russia's friendship help France?
2. If Austria-Hungary attacked Russia, how could France's friendship help Russia?
3. If Russia attacked Germany, how could Austria's friendship help Germany?

B. This British cartoon was drawn in 1904. A German general is looking surprised and worried because he cannot break a rock by kicking it.

Do a piece of writing about the cartoon explaining what you think it meant. Try to deal with the following points as you write:
1. What is the rock meant to be?
2. Why does the general want to smash it?
3. Why did he think he could smash the rock just by kicking it?
4. Why is the general worried that the rock is still in one piece?

SOLID.

GERMANY. "DONNERWETTER! IT'S ROCK. I THOUGHT IT WAS GOING TO BE PAPER."

C. Look back at what you have read about the rulers of Great Britain, Germany and Russia on pages 2, 4 and 6. Is there anything there which makes you surprised that Germany was in an alliance opposed to Britain and Russia?

7
PLANNING FOR A WAR – AT SEA

HMS Dreadnought

One cause for quarrel between the alliances was to do with the size and power of their armed forces, especially their navies.

On 10 February 1906, just a year and a day after they started building it, the shipmakers at Portsmouth Dockyard watched a battleship named **Dreadnought** slide majestically from the slipway into the sea. This event was important for two reasons. First, *Dreadnought* was the most powerful battleship ever built. Second, its revolutionary design made all other battleships out of date.

What was so different about *Dreadnought*? Partly it was that she was faster and more thickly armoured than any other warship. More importantly, she was designed to fight at long range. Her ten huge guns could blow up an enemy ship from 32 kilometres away. This made ships with smaller guns useless because they would never be able to get close enough to *Dreadnought* to fire them. German sailors soon began to call their own ships 'Five Minute Ships' because they thought five minutes was all that *Dreadnought* would need to sink them.

The Anglo-German naval race

The launching of *Dreadnought* was the latest step in a 'naval race' between Britain and Germany. The race began in 1900 when the **German Navy Law** ordered the building of forty-one battleships and sixty cruisers. Germany's naval chief, Admiral Tirpitz, also set up a **Naval League** to encourage the German people to take more interest in the navy. People were given tours of the German ports and lectures about the fleet were given all over Germany.

Britain's naval chief, Admiral Fisher, followed in Tirpitz's footsteps. More battleships were built in Britain and a **Navy League** was formed. But when *Dreadnought* was launched in 1906 it was Tirpitz who then imitated Fisher. In great haste, German shipbuilders began work on *Rheinland*, the German version of *Dreadnought*. Fisher replied to this in 1911 by building *HMS Neptune*, a 'super-Dreadnought' with more guns and greater speed. In 1913 he launched an even more powerful ship, *HMS Queen Elizabeth*; she had eight 15-inch (381-mm) guns and sixteen 6-inch (152-mm) guns.

By 1914, when war began, Britain seemed to have won the 'naval race'. Germany had seventeen Dreadnought-class battleships while Britain had twenty-nine.

This account of a naval exercise in 1912 written by Winston Churchill gives you a good idea of the tremendous power of the British Royal Navy:

'We made a great assembly of the Navy this spring of 1912 at Portland. The pennants of 150 ships were flying together. One day there is a long cruise out into the mist, dense, utterly baffling – the whole Fleet steaming together all invisible, keeping station by weird siren hootings. It seemed incredible that no harm would befall. And then suddenly the fog lifted and the whole long line of battleships, coming one after another into view, burst into tremendous flares of flame and hurled their shells with deafening explosions while the water rose in tall fountains. . . . The speed is raised to 20 knots. Streaks of white foam appear at the bow of every vessel. The land draws near. The foreign officers I have with me stare anxiously. We still steam fast. Five minutes more and the Fleet will be aground. Four minutes, three minutes. There! At last. The signal! Every anchor falls together; their cables roar through the hawser holes; every propeller whirrs astern. In 150 yards, it seems, every ship is stationary. Look along the lines, miles this way and miles that, they might have been drawn with a ruler. The foreign observers gasped.'

Why was there a naval race?

The naval race began because Kaiser Wilhelm wanted Germany to become a great world power. To achieve this, he needed a navy that could challenge Britain's navy, the largest in the world. It didn't have to be bigger, just big enough to be a threat. The idea behind this was that the British navy would stay in port rather than risk being badly damaged in a battle with the German fleet. The Germans called this the **'risk theory'**.

Britain, however, was not prepared to allow this build-up of the German navy. Britain needed a large fleet to protect her colonies and the trade routes to them. So the British naval chiefs decided to make the Royal Navy equal in size to the two strongest navies in the rest of Europe put together. This was known as the **'two-power standard'** and the idea was to have a fleet so big that no other navy would ever dare attack it.

HMS Dreadnought

Work section

A. Study the picture above and the diagrams below and read the information about each battleship. Use this evidence to write an account of how *HMS Dreadnought* was superior to all other battleships afloat in 1906.

HMS Duncan
(A pre-Dreadnought class of battleship)

Weight   13,500 tonnes
Size   123 metres long
        23 metres wide
Guns   four 12-inch (305-mm) guns
        twelve 6-inch (152-mm) guns
Armour   76mm thick
Fuel   coal
Range   4830 kilometres
Crew   720 men

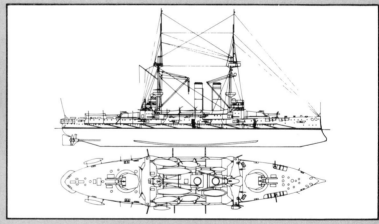

HMS Dreadnought

Weight   17,110 tonnes
Size   149 metres long
        25 metres wide
Guns   ten 12-inch (305-mm) guns
Armour   100mm thick
Fuel   coal and oil
Range   10,650 kilometres
Crew   695 men

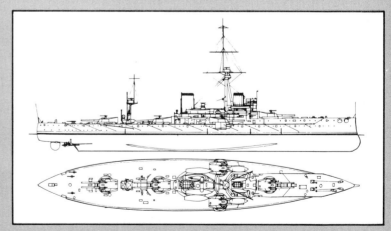

B. Read again the account by Winston Churchill of the navy exercises in 1912.
  1. What two things seemed to him dangerous about the exercise?
  2. Why do you think such dangerous exercises were carried out?

C. 1. How many Dreadnought class battleships did Germany have in 1914?
  2. Do you think Germany had enough of them for the 'Risk Theory' to be successful? Explain your answer.

PLANNING FOR A WAR – ON LAND

The Schlieffen Plan

In December 1905, while the shipmakers in Portsmouth were hard at work on *HMS Dreadnought*, an ageing German general was putting the finishing touches to a plan of war. His name was Count Alfred von Schlieffen, the most senior general in the German army.

Schlieffen was not at that moment intending to go to war. He was simply working out how Germany could fight her enemies if ever it became necessary.

As you know, Germany's main enemies were France and Russia, and this is what made Schlieffen's task difficult. If Germany fought France, Russia would attack Germany from the east. To protect the country, Schlieffen would then have to split his army into two and fight a war on two fronts – east and west. No general wants to do this because he can only use half an army to fight each enemy.

The plan that Schlieffen made in 1905 aimed to avoid a war on two fronts. He said that although the Russian armies were big, the roads and railways in Russia were so bad that the Russians would take six weeks to get into position for fighting Germany. So if war began, the whole German army should invade France by travelling at high speed through Belgium

and northern France to capture Paris. Having defeated France within six weeks, the German army would then be sent to the other side of Europe to fight the Russians who would still be getting ready.

It was a simple plan but unfortunately it really made a war on two fronts even more likely. Schlieffen took it for granted that if Russia attacked Germany, France would also attack. But suppose that France decided *not* to help Russia, and to keep out of the war, the Plan meant that Germany would attack France anyway. Schlieffen had made sure that any war fought by Germany would be a big one.

Plan Seventeen

As you will remember, the French wanted revenge against Germany for their defeat in the Franco-Prussian War. Ever since then, the French generals had planned what to do in another war – this time to win it.

They made many plans and threw out many more. Finally, in 1913, General Joffre, the French army chief, came up with Plan Seventeen.

Plan Seventeen was very simple indeed. If war broke out, the French army would make an all-out attack on Alsace and Lorraine. After capturing the two

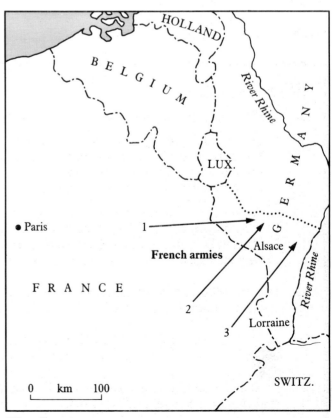

The Schlieffen Plan

Plan Seventeen

The German army practising battle tactics in 1912

'lost provinces' they would cross the River Rhine and head for Berlin. Like Schlieffen's plan, Plan Seventeen would only work if the French moved at high speed. So soldiers were trained to fight hard and furiously, to attack the enemy whatever the odds.

Other plans

In 1906 the British War Minister, Richard Haldane, agreed to help the French if ever there was a war with Germany. He therefore set about improving the British army. He formed an **Expeditionary Force** of 144,000 soldiers whose task would be to travel quickly to France as soon as war was declared. To back them up he created a **Territorial Army** of volunteers. And to make sure that there would be a good supply of officers to lead this enlarged army, he set up **Officers Training Corps** for older pupils in schools.

Both Russia and Austria-Hungary had their war plans too. Russia started to build up her armies in 1909, while the Austrians secretly made enormous cannons in their Skoda arms factory.

Well before 1914, then, the rival alliances were armed to the teeth and ready to fight each other using detailed plans for high-speed attacks.

Work section

A.   In 1911 General von Moltke of the German army wrote this about the Schlieffen Plan:

'It may safely be assumed that the next war will be a war on two fronts. Of our two enemies, France is the most dangerous and can prepare the most quickly. . . . I agree with the basic principle of opening the war with a strong offensive [*attack*] against France . . . with weak forces against Russia. . . . This is only possible by means of an advance through Switzerland or Belgium.'

1. What did Moltke mean by 'a war on two fronts'?
2. Why do you think Moltke thought that 'of our two enemies France is the most dangerous'?
3. Most of Belgium is flat, while most of Switzerland is mountainous. Can you think of a reason why the Germans decided to attack France by moving through Belgium instead of Switzerland?

B.   Between 1900 and 1914 Germany increased the number of her railway lines leading to Belgium from nine to sixteen. Look at the map of the Schlieffen Plan and suggest why this was done.

C.   Look at the map of General Joffre's Plan Seventeen. Why do you think he planned to invade that particular area of Germany? Look back to page 10 if you are unsure.

D.   Look at the photograph of German soldiers practising battle tactics. Using the information you have read about the Schlieffen Plan, say what you think the purposes of this battle practice might have been.

19

9

TWO TESTS OF STRENGTH

So far you have seen that the great powers of old Europe got into a dangerous situation by making alliances and plans for war against each other. The more they armed themselves, the more nervous and scared they became and this in turn led to further quarrels. Two serious quarrels flared up in Morocco, a country in north-west Africa. There the great powers tested each other's strength.

The Tangier Crisis, 1905

In 1905 the French were getting ready to make Morocco into one of their colonies. Britain, Spain and Italy had no objection but the Germans had not been asked for their opinion. Kaiser Wilhelm pretended that he was offended and went in person to Tangier, one of Morocco's main cities.

Mounted on a white stallion and dressed in one of his most splendid uniforms, Wilhelm rode through cheering crowds while brass bands played and rifle salutes echoed down the crowded streets of Tangier.

He then delivered a message to the Sultan (ruler) of Morocco, saying that he would stop the French takeover. As the news of this spread, people all over Europe wondered whether it would mean war between Germany and France.

In fact, Kaiser Wilhelm had no real interest in helping the Moroccans. His aim was to test the French government, to find out whether it would declare war on Germany. Even more important, he wanted to see whether Britain, France's new ally, would come to her aid.

For several weeks British and French politicians talked anxiously about what they should do. In the end they decided against war. Instead they would settle the matter at a conference to be held in the Spanish town of Algeciras.

The Algeciras Conference (1906)

The conference was a great disappointment to Kaiser Wilhelm. It decided that France could have special rights in Morocco, even though she could not have it as a colony. But Wilhelm had found out what he

Kaiser Wilhelm's soldiers riding through the streets of Tangier in 1905

wanted to know; that Britain and France would stand together against German threats while they were at the conference table, but would not join together to fight against Germany.

The Agadir Crisis, 1911

Five years later, Kaiser Wilhelm interfered again in the affairs of Morocco.

In 1911 Moroccan rebels attacked the town of Fez. The French government sent 20,000 soldiers to drive them out. Kaiser Wilhelm accused the French of invading Morocco and sent a warship, the *Panther*, to a small port called Agadir on Morocco's Atlantic coast.

The British government was greatly alarmed by the arrival of the *Panther* in Agadir. Britain had an important navy base nearby in Gibraltar and they feared that Wilhelm would make Agadir into a rival base for the German navy. The British navy was told to make ready for war and was sent to sea. Again it seemed that there would be war.

At the last moment Kaiser Wilhelm gave way and ordered German warships to leave Agadir. War had been avoided but the crisis had scared both Britain and Germany. The race to build Dreadnoughts became even more frantic as both countries prepared themselves for the next confrontation.

The scene of the two tests of strength in Morocco

Work section

A. Study this German cartoon drawn in 1911 and answer the following questions.
  1. a) Who is the man swimming in the sea?
     b) Which sea is he swimming in?
  2. What is the name of the boat in the bottom right hand corner of the cartoon?
  3. Why do you think the cartoonist has drawn the swimmer wearing a large mailed glove?
  4. Do you think the cartoonist agreed or disagreed with what the swimmer was doing? Give reasons for your answer.

B. When Kaiser Wilhelm went to Tangier in 1905, why do you think he doubted that Britain would help France to stand up to his threats?

C. Before going on to Part Three of this book, you might find it helpful to make notes on everything you have read so far. There is a guide to the most important points on the next page.

21

Revision guide

These notes are here to help you learn what you have read so far. You could copy them into your notebook or, if you prefer, use them as a framework for notes of your own.

A. **The Great Powers of Europe before 1914**
Great Britain: had the largest of all overseas empires, including India, Canada and much of Africa. Ruled by King George V.
Germany: a new, powerful country ruled by Kaiser Wilhelm II. Had ambitions to make Germany into the leading world power.
Russia: an enormous empire of many peoples with a huge population. Ruled by Tsar Nicholas II, the people were desperately poor and ready to rebel against him.
Austria-Hungary: a 'patchwork' empire of many discontented races ruled by the aged Emperor Franz Joseph.
France: a powerful republic with a large overseas empire. The President was Raymond Poincaré.

B. **Why the empires quarrelled**

1. The Alliance System   During the thirty-five years before 1914, the empires of Europe made a number of alliances:

> 1879 – The Dual Alliance (Germany and Austria-Hungary)
> 1882 – The Triple Alliance (Germany, Italy and Austria-Hungary)
> 1892 – The Franco-Russian Alliance (France and Russia)
> 1904 – The Entente Cordiale (Britain and France)
> 1907 – The Triple Entente (Britain, France and Russia)

The alliances split the empires into two rival 'camps':

The Triple Alliance	*The Triple Entente*
Germany	Great Britain
Austria-Hungary	France
Italy	Russia

2. Preparations for war   The two alliance systems were afraid of each other and started making plans for war long before 1914:

a) Planning for a war at sea.
> 1900 – The **German Navy Law** ordered the building of 100 new warships.
> 1905 – **HMS Dreadnought** was launched, making all other battleships out of date. This started. . .
> 1906–14 – a **'naval race'** between Britain and Germany in which Britain tried to maintain a **'two-power standard'** while Germany followed the **'risk theory'**.
> 1914 – Britain had twenty-nine Dreadnought class battleships. Germany had seventeen.

b) Planning for a war on land.
> 1905 – The **Schlieffen Plan** (German) aimed to avoid a war on two fronts by defeating France in six weeks and then turning to fight the less well-prepared Russians in the east.
> 1906 – Haldane began improving the British army. He set up an **Expeditionary Force**, a **Territorial Army** and **OTCs**.
> 1913 – **Plan Seventeen** (France) was for an all-out attack on the 'lost provinces' of Alsace and Lorraine.

3. The Moroccan Crises   The alliances tested each others' strength in
> 1905 – The **Tangier Crisis**. Britain and France stood firm against German threats at. . .
> 1906 – The **Algeciras Conference.**
> 1911 – The **Agadir Crisis** almost started a war when the German warship *Panther* was sent to Agadir, making the British fear that their rival naval base in Gibraltar was under threat.

PART
THREE
THE BALKAN POWDER KEG

THE BALKANS

land over 1000 metres

River Sava

River Danube

Black Sea

Adriatic Sea

Aegean Sea

Mediterranean Sea

0 km 300

The small town of Melnik in Bulgaria: a typical scene in the Balkans. Can you think of reasons why the Balkans were one of the poorest areas of Old Europe?

You have now seen that the great powers of Europe were preparing for war long before 1914 and that they very nearly did go to war on two occasions in Morocco. The worrying thing was that events in places like Tangier or Agadir, far from Europe, could take the great powers to the brink of an all-out war. In this part of the book you will find that they again came to the brink of war in a far-away place – not in Africa this time but in the Balkans.

Balkan is a Turkish word meaning 'mountain' and the Balkans are the poor, mountainous parts of eastern Europe, south of the Danube and Sava rivers. You can see what the area is like from the map and photograph on this page. Although the land was poor and wild, the great powers were all interested in getting control of it. Their rivalry there was so fierce that the Balkans were like a powder keg, ready to explode if a single spark fell in it. That is exactly what happened during the hot summer of 1914.

23

10

THE BALKAN PROBLEM

As you can see from the map below, Turkey ruled most of the Balkans at the start of this century. Turkey had once been a great empire, the Ottoman Empire, but now was weak; people called it 'the sick man of Europe'. As the 'sick man' weakened, it began to lose control of the Balkan peoples who often rebelled against Turkish rule.

The powerful countries surrounding the Balkans – Russia, Austria-Hungary, Italy and even Germany – were all interested in what was going on there. They realised that they could take advantage of Turkey's weakness to grab land and increase their influence in the area.

Why were these countries so interested in the Balkans?

The **Russians** had been hoping for many years to get ports on the Mediterranean Sea. This would make trade easier and, in time of war, her warships could not be 'bottled up' in the Black Sea. So Russia was looking for an opportunity to take coastal land away from Turkey.

Austria-Hungary also wanted ports on the Mediterranean. But the Austrians had another and more important reason for wanting the Balkans. As

you know, Austria-Hungary was a 'patchwork empire' of many nationalities. One of these was the Slav people. The Slavs wanted to break away from Austrian rule and form their own nation. Just across the border a nation of Slavs already existed – Serbia. The Serbians often stirred up trouble in Austria-Hungary by encouraging their fellow Slavs to rebel against their Austrian rulers. The Austrians therefore wanted to get control of Serbia and any other troublesome Slav areas before such a rebellion could start.

Germany had a different interest in the Balkans. Kaiser Wilhelm wanted to build a railway from Berlin to Baghdad in Persia where there were rich oilfields. The route of this 4000-kilometre railway would have to go through the centre of the Balkans.

Italy hoped to gain a strip of land on the other side of the Adriatic Sea so that she had control of the Adriatic.

So four powerful countries were keeping a careful watch on the Balkans, waiting for a chance to take land and gain influence there. The chance they were waiting for came suddenly in 1908.

In that year, a revolution by a group known as the 'Young Turks' caused chaos everywhere in Turkey.

The Balkan States in 1900

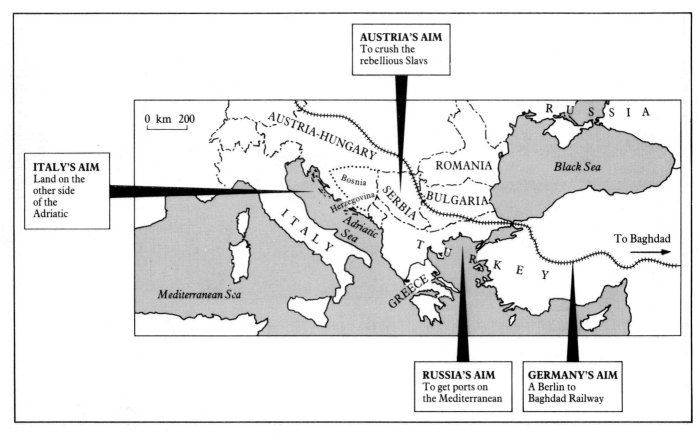

The ruler of Bulgaria (which was half-owned by Turkey) crowned himself King and declared his country independent. The people on the island of Crete broke away from Turkish rule and united with Greece.

But it was Emperor Franz Joseph of Austria-Hungary who took most advantage of this chaos in the Balkans. He seized the provinces of Bosnia and Herzegovina from Turkey and made them part of his empire.

This was a fatal mistake, however. Most of the people living in these two provinces were Serbs and King Peter of Serbia naturally claimed that they should belong to him. The people of Bosnia and Herzegovina disliked the Austrians and wanted to join Serbia. Franz Joseph had taken over a people who hated him and at the same time had made an enemy of Serbia.

The problem of the Balkans had taken a severe turn for the worse.

Work section

A. Study this French cartoon drawn in 1908 and give answers to the questions beneath.

1. a) Who is the man on the left of the cartoon meant to be?
   b) What is he doing?
2. a) Who do you think the man in the centre of the cartoon is?
   b) Why is he putting a large crown on his head?
3. a) Who do you think the figure on the right is meant to be?
   b) Why has the cartoonist made him look unhappy?

B. What do you think each of the following thought about Austria's take-over of Bosnia and Herzegovina in 1908?
   1. Tsar Nicholas of Russia.
   2. Kaiser Wilhelm of Germany.
   3. King Victor Emmanuel of Italy.
   Give reasons for your answers.

11
THE BALKAN WARS

After the Young Turk revolution in 1908 Turkey grew more and more weak. In 1911, Italy made war on the Turks, beating them easily, and this made them weaker still. The Balkan countries now saw a chance to drive the Turks completely out of Europe. The Kings of Greece, Bulgaria, Serbia and little Montenegro joined together in the **Balkan League** and in 1912 their armies attacked Turkey.

This **First Balkan War** was cruel and costly. Nearly half a million soldiers on each side fought hard and fast, and there were many atrocities. But the armies of the League proved the stronger and after just fifty

days of fighting, Turkey surrendered. At a peace conference held in London, the Turks gave up their remaining land in the Balkans and this was shared out among the four victors. In addition, a new country named Albania was created.

This was not the end of the story, however, because the four kings of the Balkan League soon began to quarrel about their shares of the land. King Ferdinand of Bulgaria wanted more land than he had been given and in 1913 he made war on Serbia and Greece in an attempt to get it.

The Balkan League

King Peter of Serbia

Highly intelligent and well educated, he had done much to improve conditions in his country.

Army = 200,000

King Nicholas of Montenegro

A fighter and a poet. His daughter was King Peter's wife.

Army = 40,000

King Ferdinand of Bulgaria

Known as 'Foxy Ferdinand', he was cunning, clever and ambitious.

Army = 300,000

King George of Greece

One of the most able and successful kings in Europe.

Army = 80,000

Turkish soldiers marching in the Balkans in 1912. Can you tell what type of unit they belonged to?

The **Second Balkan War** was a disaster for Ferdinand. Both Turkey and Romania joined in the fighting so that he found himself under attack from four sides. As a result, the Bulgarian army lost 50,000 men as well as some of the land they had gained just a year before.

The country which came out best from the two Balkan Wars was Serbia. King Peter had doubled the size of his country and his people had become more proud and aggressive. Unhappily, this made the Balkan problem even worse. The Serbs living in Bosnia and Herzegovina became restless and wanted more than ever before to belong to Serbia. The Austrians became even more worried that these people would rebel, while Ferdinand of Bulgaria grew to hate Serbia and was set on getting revenge.

The Balkans were now seething with hatred, resentment and unrest.

Work section

Compare this map of the Balkans after the Balkan Wars with the map on the opposite page. Then read the following comments which might have been made by the Balkan kings in 1913. Say which king would have made each comment.

1. 'My country has doubled in size as a result of the wars, but we still don't have any sea ports.'
2. 'I had the biggest army and we did most of the fighting, but I've been given less land than Serbia. It isn't fair.'
3. 'My country has only been given a small mountainous area next door to Serbia. It's so small it's hardly worth having.'
4. 'I'm delighted. My people are at last free of Turkish rule. We now have our own country.'
5. 'I'm quite satisfied. My country has gained extra coastland on both the Aegean and Mediterranean Seas.'

12

THE BLACK HAND AND THE MURDERS AT SARAJEVO

The Black Hand

On 22 May 1911, in the Serbian capital of Belgrade, ten young army officers formed a secret society which they named **Unity or Death**. Their leader was a twenty-six-year-old Colonel called Dragutin Dimitriević, but they knew him only by a code name – Apis. Their aim was to unite all the Slav people of the Balkans into a single country which would be called Yugoslavia. They planned to achieve this aim through the use of terrorism and the symbol of their society was to be a black hand. For this reason they were also known as the 'Black Hand'.

Before long the Black Hand had over 2 500 members, all sworn to secrecy and all sworn to lay down their lives for the cause.

Colonel Apis's first aim was to get the Serbs in nearby Bosnia under Serbian rule. He arranged that the guards on the border between Bosnia and Serbia were all Black Hand members. This meant that his terrorists could cross the frontier without fear of arrest. Once in Bosnia they could plant bombs or shoot enemies and then slip safely back into Serbia.

The Austrians, who had taken over Bosnia in 1908, were of course outraged by these activities. They feared that the Black Hand would start a rebellion in Bosnia and that this rebellion would then spread throughout their whole empire. They also suspected that the Serbian government was giving help to the Black Hand. Leading politicians in Austria advised Emperor Franz Joseph to make war on Serbia to crush this rebellion before it could even start.

In this tense situation the Austrians made a very foolish decision. They announced in the newspapers that the heir to the throne, Franz Joseph's nephew, Archduke Franz Ferdinand, would make a visit to Bosnia in June 1914. After watching army exercises he would go to Bosnia's capital, Sarajevo, on 28 June.

This newspaper announcement was foolish for two reasons. First, 28 June was the National Day of the Serbian Peoples when anti-Austrian feeling was bound to be great. Second, by giving the exact date of Ferdinand's visit to Sarajevo, the newspapers gave the Black Hand a chance to plan their greatest act of terror yet. For to kill the heir to the Austrian throne would strike a terrible blow at the country they hated.

The Black Hand quickly made plans. Three Bosnian students living in Serbia were given bombs and guns and trained how to use them. Their leader was Gavrilo Princip, just nineteen years old. Four weeks before the Archduke's visit was due to take place, the three students slipped across the border and made their way to Sarajevo.

'Apis' – the leader of the Black Hand

The Archduke's visit to Sarajevo

It was already hot and sunny when Archduke Franz Ferdinand and his wife, Sophie, arrived at Sarajevo railway station at 9.30 in the morning of 28 June. They climbed into the back seat of a large open-topped car to be driven to the Town Hall.

Crowds lined the streets as they drove through the sunny town. Waiting among the crowds were Princip and his fellow students. As the car sped along a riverside street one of them stepped forward and threw a bomb at it. Ferdinand saw the bomb coming towards him and managed to deflect it into the road where it exploded under the car behind. Ferdinand's chauffeur then sped away to the town hall.

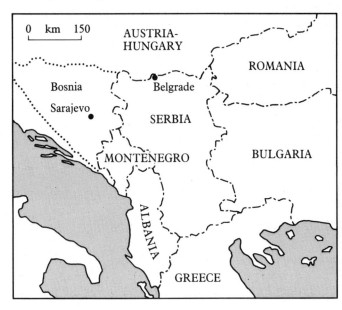

The Archduke and his wife, sitting in the back of the car, set off for Sarajevo town hall

By the time they reached the town hall, Ferdinand was furious. He shouted at the Mayor who came out to greet him and promptly cancelled the rest of the visit.

On the way back to the railway station, the chauffeur took a wrong turning. Quite by chance, Gavrilo Princip was standing in that very street. As the chauffeur reversed the car to turn it round, Princip stepped forward and fired two pistol shots into the back. One bullet hit Ferdinand in the throat: the other hit Sophie in the stomach. With blood pouring from their wounds, the royal couple were driven off at top speed to the Bosnian Governor's residence where there might be a doctor. Both died shortly after arrival.

Princip meanwhile tried to commit suicide by swallowing poison but it failed to work. He was arrested shortly after and taken to the police station where he was questioned and beaten up.

Right: A police arrest at Sarajevo on the day of the assassination. Previously historians thought the man being arrested was Gavrilo Princip, but now they believe the photograph shows another, unidentified, conspirator

Work section

A. 'Another ghastly chapter was added yesterday to the tragedy of the Royal House of Austria-Hungary. We deeply regret to announce that the Archduke Franz Ferdinand and his wife, the Duchess of Hohenberg, were assassinated at Sarajevo, the Bosnian capital.' (*Daily Telegraph*, 29 June 1914).

Why do you think the *Daily Telegraph* reporter called the murders in Sarajevo 'another ghastly chapter' in 'the tragedy of the Royal House of Austria-Hungary'? (You might find it helpful to read page 8 again before answering this question.)

B. Suppose that the weather in Sarajevo had been cold or rainy on 28 June. Might this have made any difference to the events of that day? Explain your answer.

13

THE COUNTDOWN TO WAR

The results of the Sarajevo murders

The Sarajevo murders led directly to another war in the Balkans. Franz Joseph and his advisers were sure that the Serbian government had helped the Black Hand, and decided to teach the Serbs a lesson.

One month after the murders, the Austrian government sent a long telegram to King Peter of Serbia, saying:

> 'The Sarajevo assassinations were planned in Belgrade, the arms and explosives with which the murderers were provided were given to them by Serbian officers . . . and the passage into Bosnia of the criminals and their arms was organised by the chief of the Serbian frontier service. . .'

The telegram then said that the Serbian government must take steps to get rid of the Black Hand and any other anti-Austrian societies. In addition, the Serbian government must let Austrian officials into Serbia to make sure the job was done properly. The telegram ended with these words:

> 'The Austro-Hungarian government expects the reply of the Royal Government at the latest by six o'clock on Saturday the 25th July.'

King Peter had just forty-eight hours to make up his mind and send a reply. The telegram was an ultimatum, or final demand, and if he did not agree to the Austrian demands, Austrian forces would invade his country.

Shortly before the forty-eight hour deadline was up, King Peter replied. He would do all the Austrians demanded, but with one big exception: he would not allow Austrian officials into Serbia for that would mean an end to Serbia's independence.

When they received King Peter's reply the Austrians broke off all relations with Serbia and then made their army ready for war. The next day, Austrian cannons started shelling Belgrade. For the third time in three years a war had broken out in the Balkans.

The war spreads

Before you read to the end of this story, remind yourself that the great powers of Europe were divided into two opposed alliances. Germany, Austria-Hungary and Italy were in the Triple Aliance; Great Britain, France and Russia were in the Triple Entente.

When the Austrian guns started shelling Belgrade, the Serbian government asked Russia for help. The Russians had always been sympathetic towards the Serbians because many Russians were also Slavs. So, on 29 July, Tsar Nicholas ordered the Russian army to prepare for war in order to help the Slavs of Serbia. He did not realise that this order started a countdown to the biggest war the world had ever known.

. . . 5 **Thursday 30 July**	When Kaiser Wilhelm heard that the Russian army was mobilising (getting ready for war) he sent an ultimatum to Tsar Nicholas, ordering him to stop.
. . . 4 **Saturday 1 August**	Nicholas refused to accept the ultimatum and so Germany declared war on Russia and mobilised her army. As France was an ally of Russia the French government ordered the mobilisation of the French army on the same day.
. . . 3 **Sunday 2 August**	As you know, the Germans had long ago planned how to fight a war against France and Russia. The Schlieffen Plan was to invade France through Belgium and defeat the French within six weeks before turning to fight Russia on the other side of Europe. So the Germans now started sending huge armies towards Belgium. From 6 o'clock in the morning, army trains started leaving Cologne station at the rate of one every three minutes, all heading for the Belgian frontier.

. . . 2 **Monday 3 August**	Seventy-five years before these events took place, Britain had promised Belgium that she would protect her from attack by any other country. Now that Germany was preparing to invade Belgium, the British honoured their promise. They sent a telegram to Kaiser Wilhelm ordering him to call back his army. He was given until midnight on Tuesday to reply.
. . . 1 **Tuesday 4 August**	Throughout the evening, Britain's politicians sat in the Cabinet room waiting anxiously for an answer to their telegram. One of them, David Lloyd George, recorded his feelings in these words:

> 'As the hour approached a deep and tense solemnity fell on the room. No one spoke. . . . Our eyes wandered anxiously from the clock to the door and from the door to the clock, and little was said.
> "Boom!" The deep strokes of Big Ben rang out into the night. . . . A shuddering silence fell on the room. Every face was contracted in painful intensity. "Doom!" "Doom!" "Doom!" to the last stroke. The big clock echoed in our ears like the hammer of destiny.'

No answer had come to their telegram. At midnight the operator of the telegram cable to Berlin sent off the signal GN, meaning Good Night. The line stayed dead for the next four years.

. . . 0 **Wednesday 5 August**	All the great powers of Europe were now at war with each other.

Work section

A. Read this extract from a letter written by a young Australian woman living in Germany to her sister. Note the exact date of the letter.

Leipzig 31.7.14

My Dear Emmie,

We are laying in provisions . . . I got my three tons of coal for the winter yesterday, and Fraulein Sander and I have got a hundredweight [*50 kilos*] of potatoes. Today I buy rice, macaroni, sugar and dried vegetables.

There is an extraordinary tensity in the air, work of every sort seems absolutely at a standstill, shops except the food shops, are empty, and thousands of people stand in the streets, before every newspaper office. . . .

Very much love to you all from your loving Ethel.

Now answer these questions:
1. a) What was strange about Ethel Cooper buying three tons of coal at this particular time of year?
   b) Why do you think she bought all the coal as well as so much food?
2. a) Why do you think work had come to a standstill in Leipzig?
   b) Why were thousands of people standing in front of newspaper offices?

B. Read the extracts from the Austrian telegram to Serbia on the opposite page.
   1. Judging by what you have read about the Sarajevo murders and the Black Hand, do you think the accusations made in the first extract were fair?
   2. Why do you think the Austrians only allowed King Peter forty-eight hours to reply to their demands?

C. To help you learn what you have read about in Part Three, you should now make notes on Chapters 10 – 13. There is a revision guide on the next page to help you.

31

Revision guide

These notes follow on from those on page 22. You can either copy them into your notebook or use them as a framework for notes of your own.

C. The problem of the Balkans

1. **The rivalry between the two alliance systems was made worse by the Balkan problem:**
Russia wanted to grab Turkish land in the Balkans so that she could have sea-ports on the Mediterranean.
Austria-Hungary wanted to get control of the rebellious Slav peoples in the Balkans because she feared that a rebellion in the Balkans would spread into Austria-Hungary and tear the 'patchwork empire' apart.
Germany wanted to build a Berlin to Baghdad railway through the Balkans.
Italy wanted Balkan land on the other side of the Adriatic Sea.

2. **The Balkan problem became worse in 1908 for two reasons:**
a) The 'Young Turk' revolution in Turkey caused chaos in the Balkans; e.g. Bulgaria broke away from Turkish control and declared independence.
b) Austria-Hungary took advantage of the chaos to seize the Turkish provinces of Bosnia and Herzegovina.

3. **The Balkan Wars of 1912–13**
1912 – Four kings (of Serbia, Montenegro, Bulgaria and Greece) formed the **Balkan League** and made war on Turkey.
1912 – The **First Balkan War** lasted fifty days. Turkey was beaten and her Balkan lands were divided among the four members of the Balkan League, and a new country – Albania – was created.
1913 – The **Second Balkan War** was caused by Bulgaria's ambition to get more land. Bulgaria was beaten and was left resentful and wanting revenge against Serbia.

4. **The Sarajevo murders**
In June 1914 three Bosnian students were sent by the Black Hand to kill Archduke Franz Ferdinand, heir to the Austrian throne, in the Bosnian city of Sarajevo. The murders of Ferdinand and his wife Sophie gave Austria–Hungary the excuse it wanted to take over the Balkans. On 23 July the Austrian government sent an ultimatum to Serbia. When the Serbians refused to accept part of it, the Austrian army invaded Serbia.

D. How the war in Serbia became a world war.

28 July – Serbia asked Russia for help.
29 July – Tsar Nicholas agreed to help and mobilised the Russian army.
30 July – Germany sent an ultimatum to Russia demanding a halt to the mobilisation. When Russia refused, Germany declared war on Russia. The French then mobilised their armies.
2 August – Using the Schlieffen Plan, Germany began an attack on France by invading neutral Belgium whom Britain had promised to protect.
3 August – Britain sent an ultimatum to Germany ordering a halt to their invasion.
4 August – Germany did not reply so Britain declared war on Germany.